THE STORIES I DIDN'T WANT TO TELL

LOVE, LIES & DARK CONFESSIONS

SOHINI DUTT

Made with ♥ on the Notion Press Platform
www.notionpress.com

To the broken and the brave-
the ones who bleed in silence,
the hearts that dare to love fiercely
even when the world feels cold.

This is for you.

For every scar that tells a story,
and every whispered truth that refuses to die.

May these words find you,
and may you find yourself
somewhere between the shadows and the light.

Contents

Contents

Foreword

Writing is a confession, a reckoning, a raw unfiltered bleed onto the page. These pieces are not just words; they are fragments of a soul laid bare- unmasked, unafraid, and unapologetic. This is the soul of a poet. The poet is me.

This collection is a journey through shadows and light, through passion and pain, through moments of fragile beauty and brutal truth. It is for those who dare to feel deeply, who understand that love and loss often walk hand in hand, and that the darkest nights can birth the brightest dawns. This is not the classic romance novel.

Within these pages, you will find the echoes of my heart- broken, mended, and forever searching. I do not promise comfort. I promise honesty. I promise a story that lingers long after the last word is read.

Welcome to the unrest.

Preface

This collection is not for the faint-hearted. It is a mirror cracked and bloodied, reflecting the raw, tangled mess of human emotion. Here lies the chaos behind love's pretty facade- the ache, the fury, the vulnerability disguised as strength.

I write because silence suffocates. Because sometimes the only way to survive is to bleed words onto paper. These stories and poems are the ghosts that haunt my nights and the fire that fuels my days. If I'm a writer, I'm shaped by my experiences.

If you enter these pages expecting comfort, you will find none. But if you seek truth- brutal, unfiltered, and fiercely honest- then step inside. This is where my scars speak. This is where the darkness breathes.

Brace yourself. This is my soul untamed.

Acknowledgements

To my parents and brother- thank you for being my unshakable foundation. Your love, patience, and quiet strength have carried me through every doubt and every fear.

To my close friends Yogita, Shatakshi, Niharika and Astha- my ex-roommates turned lifelong supporters — your encouragement and unwavering belief in me have been a constant light in the darkest moments. I'm grateful beyond words for your presence in this journey.

To my partner- who never let me quit, who pushed me to keep fighting when I wanted to fall- this book is as much yours as it is mine. Your fierce love and relentless faith in me have been my greatest motivation.

Thank you all for walking this path with me, for holding my hand when I needed it most, and for believing in the stories I needed to tell.

Prologue

This is not a book for the faint-hearted.

Within these pages lie fragments of a soul unguarded, bleeding truths stitched together with raw emotion and whispered secrets.

Each line is a pulse- sometimes steady, sometimes erratic- of love, pain, and the shadows lurking beneath desire.

Here, you will find the quiet battles fought in the silence of night, the twisted beauty of imperfect hearts, and the vulnerability that most hide from the world.

These words were born from moments when the world cracked open and darkness spilled in, not to consume, but to reveal.

If you dare to step inside, prepare to confront the uncomfortable, to feel the ache of honesty, and to witness love in its most flawed, fierce, and fragile forms.

This is my confession.

This is my story.

Welcome to the edge.

CHAPTER ONE

EXHIBIT A: HIM.

Consider this a detailed prompt for a masterpiece that comes to life

From the hands of a skilled painter who worships art and memorises colors.

I'm talking about this dusky-skinned boy I met a year ago

He is tall but not taller than a skyscraper

Yes, I was only a dwarf with cranberry-tinted hair and a stone-cold glare.

His eyes are deeply raw and modest, as if those pupils had been holding on to emotional, powerful stories

His voice changed moods like a chameleon changes color- sometimes husky, sometimes smooth.

His mind has been the most alluring to me,

It brims with knowledge of every kind, and yes, he understands.

I'd crown him as the King of Patience, for it's a daunting task to withstand my outbursts,

That's a virtue I've yet to tame.

His way of being is an art; I've not seen men act in love.

His smile is angelic. Simply divine.

As if resembling the glimmering light of the morning

sunshine after the darkest night of nightmares.

His anger is surprising; it adjusts. Not quick to perform.

That reminds me of control; that's a blessing to have.

His affection screams truthfulness. He loves deeply and faithfully.

The search was arduous- but somehow, it led me to him.

And my smile returned, after I handed him the reins of my heart.

Ever since, he has cradled it with fondness and care, cautious of unwanted damage.

Now it beats steady- finally fooled by something real.

CHAPTER TWO

How I Lost Him and Learned to Beg for a 'Yes.

I like to watch your face turn into shades of bright golden, as the glimmering rays of the morning sun peep in through the bedroom curtains. Your jet black, silky hair eventually appears a tinge of shining brown, and I cannot help but admire how adorable you look as you continue to sleep like a teenage boy, tired after school and play.

I like how your rough but warm hands make their grip on mine, as we walk mindlessly through the half-empty streets in the evening, as little children play soccer at a distance, and aged folk form opinions on our college love.

I like how you carefully scan through all the flavors as we stand in front of that ice-cream truck, and scratch your head asking me about my choice, even though my conventional reply would always be chocolate. I like how in the past few months I've happily settled for butterscotch, and you've made me reconsider my obsession for bonbon.

I like how you stare at me lovingly, as you slowly smoke your cigarette, and the rain keeps pouring cats and dogs outside. As the chilly gusts of wind cause my lips to tremble in cold, and hands almost feel frozen, your warm breath and that sudden bear hug, feels oh so comforting, as I thank my stars for this kind of intimacy.

Each time we sit together gulping down glasses of whiskey or vodka, I eagerly wait to get submerged in intoxication, only so I can blurt out every little way in which your love makes me feel butterflies in my belly. I know that alcohol never dominates you, and even though at times it can surely annoy, there is a certain kind of fun however in spitting out the stupidest of feelings and baby love as your man simply stares at you sober, absorbing all of the ways in which you express your affection for him.

I like how you occasionally rebuke me whenever needed, as I make a face, embarrassed to be admonished in public. But then you'd slowly whisper to me, and tell me it's just so I learn what's right, and for a moment I spot a confidant in you.

I like how you'd pull me close in public, to ensure I'm safe and protected, and somehow my face would blush red as I'd watch my dream boy do it all for me. In the nights when we'd talk about friends, family, and life, and I'd be the only one to keep blabbering like a parrot, since I talk way too much, I'd let out a coy smile as I'd watch you close your eyes every now and then, struggling hard to fight away the inevitable rush of sleep.

I like how you unnecessarily burden yourself with the silliest thought of what I should have for breakfast, even when you would battle with your hunger as your stomach would wrench in pain, and you'd keep quiet about it so gracefully. I like how your little eyes flood with tears of love, whenever I joke about leaving you. Even though I hate to see you in pain, those tears remind me of how deep our connection has grown up to be.

I'd record you when you eat, I'd record you when you laugh, but I'd rather keep my phone aside and watch you like a crazy romantic when you stand facing the mirror, and fix up your oh so gorgeous hair, and I grin from ear to ear like an idiot mad in love.

As this night marks the third day of us not talking to each other, I do open up the recordings to hear your voice, and watch your face, but nothing can really make up for this empty void that has been existing inside of me. A voice inside me says it craves for your presence.

Even though I fight, and scream obscenities, I'm sure you would know the weakest of men hide behind their anger. Anger acts like a shield that camouflages all insecurities, but alas it doesn't realize the extent to which it can cause damage. I know I've caused brutal damage, but I know it's only me who can clear up the mess that I have created.

All I'm in need of is a 'yes' that is wrapped in reassurance, and a smile that is willing to welcome me back into your world, and make me your centre.

I'll rather wait than let go.

CHAPTER THREE

THE HAUNTING TRUTHS NO ONE TELLS YOU ABOUT HEARTBREAK.

Walking down the same old deserted street, I realize I am no longer the same old me. Although the neighborhood looked familiar, and a strong gust of wind brought back month old memories that I had been saving myself from, I could sense a part of me no longer existed like it used to once. I look ahead and continue walking, foolishly wondering if I'd spot you at a distance, waiting for me to come hold your hand. I can feel a teardrop escape my already moist eyes, but this time I don't sense any need to wipe it off. I'm too fragile to withstand the overwhelming outpour of intense emotions. I can smell meat being cooked somewhere, but nothing delights me anymore. Perhaps it is the sour realization that this time I'd have to finish it all alone. Young lovers in and around the corners makes my heart palpitate, as if I had summoned anxiety to settle in. I look at them smile at each other, as they rest their heads upon their lover's chest, and an empty void within me yearns for attention. I just cannot fathom if it is the affection that I crave, or is it the simple assurance of having you right beside me whenever I was close to crumbling. Isn't it utterly unfair that you spent the longest of days and nights with me, fulfilling every fantasy that I ever dreamt of, only to turn them into memories that haunt me as nightmares each time I force my eyes shut? Isn't it insanely cruel of you to touch me in the ways that no one ever could; only so one morning I'd plead my stars to let me feel your warmth for one last time? Isn't it brutal of you to talk of a shared future in which I'd be the hot-tempered mother of your kids, only to leave me midway wondering if our love had been so delicate? Let me tell you just so you know, falling in love hasn't been easy. I knew it would be one rollercoaster ride, but I was prepared to embrace the thrills. Waking up next to you each morning soothed my senses beyond your imagination. I'd only care about keeping happy, because everything else magically fell into place. All the random cups of tea by the roadside stalls, silly comments hurled at strangers, slurping spicy noodles at the same old shop (because you knew I'd never opt for anything else), smoking cigarettes in the breezy evenings, exchanging playlists while you'd mock my tastes, teasing me with your friends while I would blush and hide my face, giving me life lessons that shaped me into a woman of power, all those late night rides while the rain poured down on us, kissing underneath the stars while your creepy neighbor watched us silently- I never wished for these to turn into faint memories that I'd narrate to a friend at three in the morning, with bright red eyes devoid of sleep, as I'd rub them time and again, and speak through my tears. Isn't it heartless of you to lift me up like a princess and give me a glimpse of the world we both could inhabit, only to suddenly decide to drop me from such a height so I fall into rock bottom, and never see you again? Is that what love is all about- quitting when there's no meeting point? I still wonder.

Just a week back, I found myself around some great company- young men who were equally broken into shreds and pieces, yet stood through to carry on with the life they've envisioned to live for. They watched me fall but stood right there to pick me up. They then pushed me harder so I'd fall even worse, but then asked me to pick myself up. They showed me what love felt like, but they also told me about the powers it came with. They warned me that love could build you, but break you too. They shared with me their biggest secret- that no matter how happy you saw a man to be, every man carries a lonely heart that longs for acceptance- the acceptance of a man who could crumble at times, who could collapse anytime whenever the load of responsibilities would weigh heavy on him. They taught me that life helps us grow, life helps us understand. It is the toil and struggle of life that gives us the perfect shape. They taught me that heartbreak is universal.

But even then there are nights when I jump back into the thoughts of us, letting myself weep profusely as my heart slowly accepts the absence that you've left behind. I still feel empty and wasted, I still feel devoid of emotions. I still look for love in every boy that smiles back at me, I still look for assurance in every man that embraces me. I still think of heartbreak when someone confesses his liking for me. I still search for you when someone mentions love to me. If not as my Prince Charming who'd ride his white horse to carry me to his castle, won't you ever meet me at the other end of the river, as a friend I'd never want to part ways with? If not love and the apocalyptic romance, can we not sit on the moist grass and simply talk about how once we blissfully enjoyed existing together? Can we not cry in each other's arms, as we'd barely be able to breathe, until one of us cracks a joke and both of us break into laughter, only to realize we still love each other like we used to?

CHAPTER FOUR

A Raw Confession You'll Relate To.

Hello, you.

I would've preferred to keep my story wrapped in silence,
But maybe tonight serves as that distinct moment of weakness—
Disguised as a reminder for self-introspection.
And I have chosen to let its power consume me.
I possess a body filled with shrieks and screams
And all other kinds of voices that only I hear—
Not the world I'm in.
Ironically, my exterior presents my personality
As the calmest entity—
One that chooses to "beast out" only when overwhelmed with vulnerability.

Tomorrow summons yet another sunny day,
With the scorching heat inflicting extreme infuriation onto me.
I'll wake up with swollen eyes,
Begging me in desperation to find my way back to the bed.
I'll force my degrading body to muster up
Whatever strength remains,
So I can survive a shower
And look at myself in the mirror—
Before I camouflage under several shades of bronze and blush
To "contain" my facade before the world.
I'll act as if I'm always given so much attention
That I barely get to lend myself a few seconds to recover.
As would be evident from the fake phone call I continue to be on
Until I get a means of transport
To the 10-minute-away subway station.
Once inside, I'll attract a handful of gazes—
Wanted ones, maybe.
I like to think the world values my presence wherever I go,
No matter how overwhelmingly discomforted I feel
The minute I catch their glaring eyes on me.
Until I find a seat
And begin my feeble attempts at distraction—
Shifting my crooked attention
To an unsolved murder mystery online.
I'll enter through the gigantic glass doors,
Assure myself I'll certainly leave for home on time.
A lie I repeat, daily.
Sitting at my desk,
Eyeing the screen,
Fidgeting,

Cursing myself for taking such a long route
To reach somewhere
Just because it offers me financial validation.
    I catch sight of a few familiar faces here and there.
They'll wave at me, and I'll wave back with a stretched smile,
Knowing completely well—
I'll never have myself like them.
    And just then, I'm reminded—
My well-wishers (I like to call them that,
For the sake of my satiation and ego)
Keep reaching out whenever they can,
Even amidst their own messes.
    All I manage to do
Is enjoy the attention—
Not begged for, but granted nevertheless.
    Where's the harm in wanting to feel important
When you've seldom had that privilege?
    The problem arises when I let my mind slip aside,
Abandoning the thought
Of ever replying back.
    As a writer, I hold on to a massive repertoire of stories—
All of which find their way back
To my thought process,
To the way I function
To view life.
    I consider these pages my safest haven—
They bear all my secrets,
Dark enough for a normal human to digest
Without a pinch of salt.
    These blank pages do not second-guess.
They give me endless space
To share or vent

Whatever is destroying the remnants of my sanity.
      And so, I see this world
As harboring the most selfish humans
Mankind could've ever witnessed.
      Relationships are both conditional and transactional.
Therefore—
The moment a person
(Disguised as the closest friend,
Or the beloved Prince Charming on a white horse)
Gets closer,
I shut the door in their face
And tighten the lock to my fragile heart—
So they cannot destroy what's already broken.
      Rising back from the ashes
Is only a beautiful phrase in fiction.
Reality has other ways to teach you.
      I get bored—
Of the same face,
The same work,
The same outfit,
The same story.
      Death entices me.
Dread excites me.
Misery pleases me.
      Truth be told,
Happiness is only a myth
Crafted by delusional writers of romance.
So, the false existence of it enrages me.
      I've learnt—
Living is not something each deserves.
Not every face is friendly.
Not every place is inviting.
Not every favor is unconditional.

Not every relationship is family.

The mirror won't flinch, the screen won't care, the world won't wait.

And with this lesson,
I'm prepared to wake up tomorrow—
And carry myself with false niceties.
Because if I'm to survive with relationships,
I need to shake hands with enemies

CHAPTER FIVE

A Raw Confession That Might Change How You See Love.

Am I falling for you? As a naïve young man who is yet to decipher my inner self, only so he can boldly claim my heart, tonight is your time for I'm about to enlighten you with stories that have written down my existence. If you trust yourself as a careful listener, consider it a test of your potential as one. May I also mention, that although you've repeatedly reminded me of your non-judgmental character, tonight I ask for it? You must listen to all that my heart has held on to, ever since my eyes met yours, and how it has struggled since to carefully note down every detail and feel every emotion, before it is prepared to set out for a new adventure, which someday might also lead us to wake up next to each other, not as plain romantic lovers, but as partners bonded by the ring of love. You ask me if it is love that I feel for you. Surely, it is a strong emotion, but I choose to ask you, what do you know of love? What do you think it is? Tonight let me tell you how a hopeless romantic and a devoted lover as me think it to be. Love to me is the soothing comfort you feel as you lay your head against his chest, after a rigorous day at work. Love to me is when you look at him smiling, and you know it's a good day. Love to me is when you collapse every minute, but he is willing to pick you up again. Love to me is when it's just the howling winds, and a peaceful lane devoid of people, as the birds circle the clear blue horizon, and suddenly nothing seems colorless but full of life, soulful. Love to me is when there is joy in silence, with him by your side. Love to me is when you cry, and loathe, as you snort and your nose turns red, and your eyes hurt from all the tears, and he still sits in silence watching you, for you're still a child in his eyes. Love to me is when your failures don't scare him, and tells you they are the stepping stones, and that he'd walk alongside you. Love to me is the realization, that this man is my refuge, and the day the world caves in on me, he would be waiting on the other side, with a reassuring smile. Love to me, is the faith that amidst all the worst and dread, he would never abandon me, for we are all we have for each other. You may wonder what makes me different. You see, these words and paragraphs aren't my way of making you fall for my naïve and teenaged heart, but a conscious attempt of mine to let you see the spent soul in me that still longs for a man like you. Think of me as an unfortunate child who loves like an artist loves his art, or the ether loves the rain, yet was never exposed to the pure form of affection that is unfiltered, selfless, patient, and liberal. Think of me as the mislead lover who thought it was real whenever a random man gave her the least possible. Think of me as an exhausted little one, who still longs for a love that never abandons her when she leaves her heart bare. Think of me as the personification of permanence, and I promise to never deceive you, for I know the pain of betrayal, just like a soldier knows the hurt of wounds in a battle. You see I wasn't born as a crazy romantic. However I knew love drove you crazy. Although you do feel your heart pounding when his face resembles sheer divinity, what keeps you holding on to them is how you catch yourself smiling whenever they smile. I had a 'first time' when someone said he loved me. But as I grew up, I reckoned not everyone realizes what love really is. Either it happens only once, or it doesn't fade away in a few months. That was the day I discerned that attraction was not love. Real love never ends, it either exists somewhere in the corner of your heart, or consumes you entirely. If today, you don't love the same, it was never love to begin with. The day you spoke to me, I didn't pay heed to your words, and how they beautifully escaped your soft lips, and sounded like music to my ears. What I rather was attentive towards, is how grown you were as a person with emotions. I would rather confess that I did want to kiss you, but my racy and disobedient heart had other plans. It demanded patience and guided attention. It was immensely curious to test your endeavors, and it wanted to affirm whether you were the man I had dreamt of as a teenage kid. I can't tell if love had already begun to bloom, but I am certain the foundations were laid. To know of your being, I never needed a zillion hours. You seemed so crystalline to me, I could read you through your eyes, and write you with your words. You surely are a curious man, and I wouldn't shy away from saying that it did pull me towards you, but not entirely. I sensed a similarity in our pain. I sensed a resemblance in our personalities. You were tired, and I was too. Was it time that we needed each other? That dull-witted heart screamed a 'yes!', but I rebuked it in response. "Patience", I reminded myself, and continued to test you in words. And just like that, days would pass by, and you would occasionally write to me, but you never spoke to me. Your fingers typed countless phrases, but your heart kept silent, as if cautious of any colossal damage. And I'd smile, realizing how you resemble me so well. Yet, you see, I am an author. And although not all readers are writers, all writers certainly read. And I read through your utterances. Although in the initial days, it hurt me to see you admire my appearance and not my soul; I questioned myself asking how you could anyway, when it was scarred by the ravages of time. But that was until one blissful evening, you told me you wanted me to stay. I vividly recall myself blushing beyond limits, merely staring at my phone's screen, as you continued to type in intervals. My face would flush red, and my grin wouldn't stop, as I constantly covered my face with my right hand, foolishly imagining you standing in front of me, watching me go crimson for you! And so my love, the scene was set, the script was written, and the final edit was eagerly awaited for. And it all came to materialize on the 14th of December, the night I just didn't want to let go of you. That night I was certain my intuitions had not lied. The Universe was giving me another chance to let go of all my miseries, and be blissfully in love with you, truly, madly, deeply. But now is the time I tell you that I come with a disclaimer. Tell me dear love, how do you heal a bruise that has become black with time? Do you think the bare minimum would suffice, or extra care is demanded when situations grow worse? I don't ask you to be my physician and write me prescriptions for the rest of my life to follow, but if I may, cant I ask you to be that aid that would be there for me, whenever the pain grew severe? If you fall a hundred times, I'd pick you a thousand times. If love is a poem, I am the poet. If love is a song, I am the singer. If love is an illness, I am the patient. If love is an accident, I am the victim. If love is a muse, I am the dreamer. If love is an art, I am the painter. So if to me, love is you, I am your beloved. I have never fancied abandonment, and of that I'm certain. But if tonight I decide to make you my home, would you choose to reside in it? I'm in two minds.

CHAPTER SIX

You're Not Here to See It.

Day 15 of writing a letter to you,

Just some twenty minutes ago, I had posted a picture of me online. If only we were still connected, I'm certain you would've smiled looking at it. I smile in that picture. The agonizing beam of the glowing afternoon sun casts a brownish golden tint in my eyes. My pale yellow skin is glistening in the sunshine, as I smile for the picture. My hair feels smooth and healthy, as it rests calmly on my shoulders, unbothered by the wild breeze. I know you'd have been happy to hear about this day, because I made a new friend. I vividly remember how you said, "good people make good friends. You just need to find them". Well, she had always been a bosom buddy, but this afternoon she had been my custodian. She had been a keeper of my little secrets, and the sole witness to my bruised existence. If only a friend of yours would share this picture with you, you'd get to see how lively I look! Yes, I haven't cried. I haven't mourned for your absence. I haven't laid my emotions bare, and I haven't cursed my love for you. On the

flipside however, I talked to her about you, and how we'd have been if you had been here with me. The place was infested with lovers of all kinds. For once in all these years, we even spotted a man of around fifty being affectionate with his wife. All of them reminded me of you, and I laughed madly. I laughed recalling how you loathed showing affection in public. I laughed recollecting how you'd ask me to rather 'behave' if I had requested you for a kiss while I lay my head on your thighs. Oh one thing you'd not be much happy about, and that is the choice of music we chose today. We didn't listen to your treasured Punjabi hits, but soft renditions of classic Bollywood. A woman walked up to us, requesting us for a picture with her lover man, to which my friend happily agreed. I shall now tell you how it reminded me of that festive night on the 1st of October, when you walked up to a cold looking, self contained man, with a similar request, and he made us look like some billed platypus having a rough day.
Oh how I missed you today, if only you knew.

Your friends no longer talk to me. I thought they had become my friends too, but perhaps four months were not long enough for them to build a bond with me. I never knew friendships were way more vulnerable than thriving hearts. If only they liked me like they used to once, perhaps you could see that I'm doing good. I still smile, and I still pose for pictures. I wore your favorite clothes, and the shoes that you always wanted to get for me. Don't worry, for you won't see me grieve you. I know you wanted me to be a strong woman, and I'm on my way to become one. Perhaps watching me love myself more than I have loved you, would someday bring you back to me. I had a wonderful evening. I hope you did too.

CHAPTER SEVEN

Why We Keep Falling for Love, Even When It Breaks Us?

Many of us are hopeless romantics, always looking for the 'fairytale love' that we see in movies, and read in conventional and idealistic poetry. Even though barely a possibility, we still like to believe in the idea that someday such a love would be achievable. People like us just can't think of a life that is deprived of romantic love, and the thrill of commitment, even when we are ourselves on the edge of life, so much so that we are certain one wrong step would cause us to fall off the cliff, and it all would come falling apart. Herein lays the baffling irony, because even after knowing it all full well, we are more than willing to risk it all because somehow we wish to make believe in the idea of chances. It's a 'hit or miss' situation, and yet we embrace the daunting challenge whole heartedly. I wonder how many of us would be willing to take on such uncertain challenges when it came to equally important matters, for instance career opportunities, and establishing a stable future. Maybe this is exactly why the world says that love blinds you. So much so, that you fail to ascertain the pros and cons, and all the missed signals simply look like ongoing chances for betterment. Maybe that is what lets people like us to continue to be overwhelmed and swooning over a kind of love, which we have certainly attempted to equate with the perfected and enhanced version depicted in books, and films. Some among us are waiting to start afresh. We have never been told that we were the reason for someone's lost sleep, weirdly interesting dreams, heightened rush of adrenaline, jitter and overwhelming excitement, or even why someone never missed a class, or skipped the morning assembly. We were so oblivious of what it meant to be spending time with the special someone, that we would bury our heads in shame if they came specifically to see us. We would be drowning in the sea of awkwardness when a friend would catch someone staring at us, and smiling. People like us would grow up to be so conscious of ourselves in terms of appearance and confidence, that at times we would look into the mirror and pause for a moment to point out the visible flaws that might've kept them away. And just then, a friend would come to hold your hand, and look you in the eye, with an assuring smile and a firm grip, to tell you that you're perfect just the way you are, only so you continue to hold on to the sliver of hope within, that someday someone would be eager to see you right after the morning sun disturbs their peaceful slumber. We do wait for that 'romantic love' but at the same time watch it co-exist with the other aspects of life, as the saying of 'go with the flow' floods our conscience, and we know we're out of choices. There is this other group of people who are now used to falling in love, watching it eventually escalate and surpass all boundaries, and then suddenly find them doomed by the very idea of it. These people have taken care of all possible and necessary requirements to somehow try to stay afloat, as the surges of love continue to grow wild. They started out as insecure lovers, beginning to acknowledge the fact that love was a two-way process, and trust comes with a boost in confidence. They begin as half-hearted individuals who are yet to love themselves, and therefore tend to constantly rely on their partner for support. They do not realize that the only true source of their mental peace is they themselves, and their quality and ability of manifesting the same, through self-care. Yet some others find love when they are already struggling to move past their existing trauma. Then there are those who watch the spark gradually fizzle out, as the beginning had been way too intense. So much so, that now all there's left is consequent obsession, which ultimately tarnishes the essence of the bond. These people have survived through so much, that the slightest glimmer of hope ends up lightening up their faces, although now they are governed by the constant fear of abandonment, or the worry of the past repeating itself. While on the one hand, some are naïve lovers waiting to be loved and willing to give in their everything, only so they do not end up losing, and being left alone once again, the others on the other hand are already exhausted beyond possibilities, and fail to whole-heartedly embrace the new kind of love that comes to them. While giving in everything already, turns you into a foolish lover blinded by the idea of unconditional intimacy and fondness, restricting yourself on the other hand makes you yearn for acceptance and acknowledgement, even as you teach yourself to love within boundaries. The only solution to this inevitable conflict therefore, is tremendous amount of patience, and the willingness to help make it work, no matter how longer it takes. But one shall also not forget that we are part of a fast moving world, where people barely have the time to take a pause and breathe.

We certainly are a group of heightened individuals who lack the ability to have unwavering patience in them, and the willingness to wait for change. If love demands patience and readiness, then perhaps the contemporary world is yet not ready for "our" kind of love.

In a world that never stops rushing, maybe the greatest act of love is simply having the patience to wait- for ourselves, for others, and for a love that's truly ready to grow.

CHAPTER EIGHT

I WONDER IF MY ROOM MISSES ME LIKE I MISS MYSELF.

A sudden sense of discomfort irks my peaceful slumber, and I realize the morning sun has come to visit me.

With the right eye half open, and my vision yet grainy and blurry, I somehow catch a glimpse of the ticking clock on the wall in front of me; it's already half past seven. I can hear the gurgling sound of the bottles being filled, sloshing of water into bowls, The clinging of glasses and clanging of metal, and the opening and closing of drawers; it was a sure thing that mother was up and about, and I had to start my day. Even though another week of inactivity and laziness was coming to an end, I knew the next forty-eight hours would only make it worse.

I casually pass a smile to everyone as I head to the washroom; and lock myself in after it's all done. As the clear, cold water touches my face, the sleep that burdened my eyes suddenly disappears, and I realize it's just a typical day that sunk back into its wonted routine. I brush my teeth and wash my face, and stare right at the mirror facing me. My face looks fresh, but the insides of me are all the same-devoid of enthusiasm and bereft of hope. After my first cup of steaming coffee, I walk back to my room that still looks the same.

The faded yellow curtains stand still, hanging from the rods above. The huge windows of glass are shut since morning, so the frequent breeze stays outside. My age-old study is now dust-laden, for I seldom use it to write my stories. The children novels on the shelf above wait in silence, stuck onto each other like students holding onto each other's school bags at the time of dispersal.

I wonder if the curtains liked to flutter, as and when the gusts of wind caused them to.

I wonder if the study still wishes I'd someday sit down, and work on a story like I used to. I wonder if the creaking bed liked changing its covers, or if it wished to stay the same, forever and always.

I wonder if the huge, wooden cupboards missed the clothes that I threw away when they grew old. I wonder if the windows ever wished to let the wind play with them.

I wonder if this dingy room yearned for the rays of the mighty sun. I wonder if it comes back to life, when the morning sun settles in.

I wonder if the novels wished to be re-read, in the hope that this time I might find something new.

I wonder if my schoolbags wished I wore them one last time.

I suddenly catch myself smiling, for all these thoughts appear silly. But what if they had life like us, would we share similarities? What if they could dance and sing, would they have a life better than me?

I think of the times when they heard me speak, spill out secrets, and watched me sob. I think of the days when they caught me smiling, giving life another chance. I recall the nights when they stared at me, while I lay silent and lived through confusion. I wonder if the ceiling fan was tired of constantly moving around.

I wonder if these fluffy pillows someday felt I was too heavy.

I wonder if these silent walls someday wished to speak to me.

If only still life could move and feel like us, I'm afraid I'd one day be called an extrovert.

CHAPTER NINE

THE SILENT WAR WITHIN.

These barbarous battles are often fought in silence, and I am that mighty warrior, brutally bruised yet somehow still alive.

My enemies aren't troops, or a swarm of armed militia, but a ruthless mob of thoughts, which pester me all day.

Every night when the lifeless sky comes to witness my exposed defeats, I fill my mind with perseverance, for someday I must win.

I mustn't win for any personal pride, but for him who has given me a trial. Call it a dare, but I must prove my courage, lest I'd lose his love for me.

I wasn't born a defective human, but I grew flawed with the touch of time. I believed love would heal my open sores, but I laughed when it caused them to bleed even more.

I waited and waited, even then, hoping one day my king would arrive. His sword of love would be mighty enough, to vanquish the affliction of my tormented soul.

And then one morning, I saw his face, smiling and flushed with empathy. The words were said, and my heart nodded foolishly, eager to be shattered again.

I knew I was filthy, both in soul and mind. But he called me a lunatic, and dreaded my thoughts, for he was an accomplished man- so he thought.

You may laugh at me now, but he was my only true friend. I gave him my heart and hoped he would stay.

Just when his words pricked my head like arrows, I fell like a slain soldier, crushed in the battle of love.

Yet I stood up firm, waiting for him to hold my hand, so we walked through it all together.

But he pushed me away, and I walked alone, all smashed and battered.

He gave me time, and said I must change. Baffled, I continued with the trials.

But alas, he was blind to witness my struggles, and parted his ways forever.

At times the eyes well up and daunting memories torment my sleep.

I still wake up with a broken smile, hoping someday his heart would miss mine.

CHAPTER TEN

IF EVERY DAY WAS MY BIRTHDAY.

The wind chimes played along, as the icy cold breeze danced with grace.

In a moment, the curtains joined in, fluttering in the rhythm of the wind.

I did look out once or twice, but the moonless sky remained the same. The wind was strong, and I quivered, but something within held me firm.

I glanced at the bedroom clock, which kept ticking on. A few minutes to midnight, and I'd be bombarded with calls.

I'd have to read elaborate letters, I wondered, even though I couldn't tell which words were true.

I'd wake up to the sweetest voices; I'd see my family smile at me. I'll be encircled with the brightest faces, people who would cherish my presence.

It scared me to envision such a morning, for I am not used to living it often.

I could talk, sing, and dance; I could laugh, and act nonchalant.

But what startles me is the need of a day to be marked, which read, 'It is my birthday'.

I silently walked up to my bed, as if cautious to not make a sound.

I pulled the sheets all the way to my face, as I buried myself within its layers.

The minute I felt the warmth of the fabric, a tear-drop escaped my eye, and I wept. I wept till my eyes grew sore, and sleep took over my conscience.

As per the prophecy of the previous night, I had woken up to an unusual morning. I answered calls, and thanked people; for I'm grateful they acknowledge my existence.

I watched enemies turn to genial folks, and tricksters become considerate, it was funny how one date in an entire year transformed and altered images.

I am now in my room, laughing at it all, for it's too good to be true.

They are eager for celebrations, and a cake to be cut, but all I want is for this happiness to stay.

It startles me to see, that people plan things when there aren't occasions, but their 'planning' takes a backseat when an event demands it.

It astonishes me to see, how everyone changes for the sake of one fine day, and as the sun sets in and the moon is summoned, all become same, they return to their past.

Every year, they ask me to make a wish, and I laugh at how I repeat it all.

As the dusk shifts to dawn, and I see the zeal fading out, a painful chuckle comes out, and I realize it all is short-lived.

How beautiful would it be, if each day was a celebration of our existence? for we are born just once, but we live forever, "It's my birthday", I say to myself, as if to remind me once again,

That the show must go on.

CHAPTER ELEVEN

THE LIMITS OF LOVE.

To fall in love is a universal experience. If your stomach twists and turns unusually when you see them, if your heart beat fastens its pace when they look you in the eye, and if you feel your blood rushing furiously as they let out a smile, then you must know it's love that has consumed your senses, as you reckon you're no longer able to push it back. Falling in love is that easy.

What's nightmarish however is whether that someone loves you back; whether they spot the shine in your eyes as your cheeks flush red, whether they catch sight of the momentary crease in your skin extending from both sides of your nose to the corners of the mouth as you struggle to hide the smile, and whether they sense the heightened rush of emotions in you as you get all jittery and begin feeling butterflies inside. And if they do discover it all, and sense a similar desire, then it's nothing but two lovers destined to unite. And love happens just like that- a kind of love that is driven by unfathomable passion, the consistent and overwhelming urge to see each other every day of the week, and the irresistible impulses that drive you bonkers.

A love that offers you adventure and makes you step out of the ordinary, is what pushes you to crave for it every passing day. Love intoxicates your soul to the extent that it becomes an arduous challenge to live a day without them.

I had become the fortunate victim of such a love almost three months back, and ever since not a day has passed when I didn't succumb to the cruelties of distance. Surely a favored generation, we need not wait for handwritten letters to arrive, neither do we have to strive for phone calls. However when the ever-increasing farness and the overwhelming burden of assignments keep you within bounds and confines me to limits, then how do I tame that furiously beating heart inside of me that shrieks in agony as it grieves for your absence? How do I teach it to not get nostalgic each time a day of togetherness comes to a close? How do I reason with the foolishly anxious mind of mine that just can't think of anything else but you? How do I convince my longing soul that it must not give up on hope? How do I summon all my strength to force it all into submission, when the soaring emotions in me are just not willing to listen? The day you come up with an answer to it all, I shall finally teach my heart to love in limits.

CHAPTER TWELVE

THE LAST LULLABY.

A massive, hope-filled apartment.
One fluorescent light bulb swings, causing a jagged shadow to form-
The air is thick with the stench of decay; something rotting for years now.
The stink is familiar.
The dim light illuminates my blood-soaked frame.

In the centre, lies a diary, heavy with the darkest confessions and forceful scribbles resembling careless writing.
My heart is carved open; more like a hideous bouquet.
A jarring hum fills the air. I recognize the voice.
I've always liked to sing when no one's watching.

It's a twisted lullaby this time- a conscious attempt at lulling me back to sleep.
A peaceful slumber that will last an eternity.
The blood is my canvas, and I'm now the victim.
My drowning eyes are obsession-filled, my soul has been raging in fury. Quieter though.

I hear my heartbeat drown every second, as the hand
slips off the bed's edge.
Like the missing punctuation at the end of a sentence.
I want to keep it easy this time-
So I close my eyes and prepare for the journey.

CHAPTER THIRTEEN

ILLUSIONS OF AN UNFINISHED LOVE.

Empty coffee cups lay scattered around the rusty, wooden desk.

The squeaking sound of the door hints at the gentle gusts of wind outside.

My gaze shifts to the potted money plant in the dust-choked balcony.

Its leaves are drooping, becoming limp and weak. I have sucked the life out of it too.

The clock keeps ticking, I wait for the glaring sun outside to die down.

The door slams shut, I flinch.

A murder of crows cries out- a warning.

The wind has gradually gained momentum.

A wailing sound echoing louder-

Signaling the arrival of something sinister.

I think about taking another sip of caffeine, and just then,

I spot a slow-moving shadow lurking across the wall.

I rub my eyes, turning them crimson red, swollen like a tea bag steeped too long-

I jolt upright

To realize that he is gone.

These illusions have become the curse of my unfinished love story.

CHAPTER FOURTEEN

The Cost of Comfort.

Leisure pursuits are inherently diverse. Mine however, is a conscious desire aimed at reaching a final understanding. Some call it realisation; I call it awareness: awareness that life is a colorful mosaic of the most striking colors, each hue narrating a distinct memory. Today's conscious desire was to let my mind travel back to the days when life was smoother, calmer. Not my teenage years to be specific, but certainly the time when I was younger, and all the burdensome decisions haunted my father's nights. All of us grew up listening to how digesting all the knowledge that was imparted to us would land us a coveted place in this earth populated by racing rats, running helter skelter without a vision. No one told us that to begin with, we must know how to put that insight to use. But that's another story of twisted fate.

The prime attention shifts to the nature of mounting, never-ending, often sinister, problems and how the daunting struggles of our selfless parents never let us experience the slightest discomfort of it all. Everything ran smoothly, and the hunger for amassing more, kept on soaring high. Because, obviously, our needs were met. So why not continue wishing for more?

Today when we're finally functioning as adults of this intensely competitive world, somehow landing a 9-5 job, and beginning to earn entry-level salaries, and desperately struggling to afford the bare minimum with our hard-earned money, the silent cries of our parents ring a bell loud enough for us all to hear: the silent echoes of their sacrifices. Loud. Clear. Unforgettable.

The scorching heat does not enrage you anymore, because the sky-high bills remind you of your limits and responsibilities. Meals are no longer taken for granted but a luxury to be experienced, because time slips like sand. You've traded branded clothes for home essentials- a quiet transition that reflects a more grounded, mature self. Fine dining has now become an occasional thought that comes and goes. Social circle has only been shrinking, now we barely recognize one or two faces as familiar. It's no more loud music or cheering crowds but the silence roaming around, within the four walls of your bedroom that reminds you of comfort and leisure on a weekend. Restful sleep has become a myth and the alarm has replaced your father's gentle wake-up call- and with it, so much more. You hunt down apps to keep your scattered life in line- online reminders like lifelines, tiny pings pulling your focus back to things. Yes, your mother now lives miles away- her absence echoes louder than any notification.

The world has hushed around you- you're on your own now. No one's coming. No one's calling. It's just you- and the soul-crushing weight of becoming.

You watch a car pass by and find yourself desperately wishing to own one. It's been too long- too many hours spent standing in the subway, crammed among countless others, gasping for space, as your feet turn to stone.

And then it strikes you- comfort is not offered. It's earned. Your parents earned it for you. The baton of responsibility has been transferred. Now, it's your turn to return the favor. Walk ahead with conviction and make what they call "life".

CHAPTER FIFTEEN

THE BOY WHO TAUGHT ME TO LIVE.

They talk about your favorite color, a favorite cuisine or a favorite holiday destination. And sometimes when they ask you about your favorite person, more than often you might end up naming your partner. For me however, there is a slight but significant difference here. My favorite person is no lover but a young boy who has taught me the most precious lessons that I found in no bestseller. This boy is sure young, but his demeanor is painted golden and shines bright in the dark. We have grown under the same roof but matured very differently. The same, old house saw a vulnerable young girl with unrealistic dreams succumb to the tantrums of a weak mind and inevitable shenanigans of a childish heart. While it also saw a young, timid boy who never spoke much, blossomed into a man so polished and groomed for his age, that you'd only find a similar soul described in metaphors in an old, romance novel. Both were taught the same values and given the same education.

The difference was only a minor one- the girl listened while the boy understood. Over time, the realisation steadily surfaced and it so appeared that the fanciest education or the overwhelm of life never taught us living. Life was an art that only a stable man could master; the one who knew exactly what he wanted and never wasted a second spending time in distractions. Nothing allured him except the vision of a life that he could feel proud of. And although five years younger, he taught the girl that no one can bring you down unless you let them. Back when he was younger and just a shy kid trying to settle down, in this chaotic medley called 'life', he was mocked for his body and laughed at for not being an overachiever; contrary to what this girl had been doing back then. Today, as time has passed and both have grown older, he is revered for his sense of commitment and the worship of his ongoing vision. He seldom desired luxury; an ideal birthday gift for him was just worth some pennies. And today, he has left us all this lesson that desiring luxury is every common man's personality. But becoming capable enough to afford the luxury is what defines a true visionary. Despite being the achiever of her class and getting educated in the best, the girl still loathes her choices and weeps in the embrace of confusion that her present has caused her. The boy however, laughs and rejoices in the discipline he has built for himself, even after never being the star of his class, as this sincerity has offered him the sweetest fruit that he was obsessed to have someday. He taught me to be obsessed with a goal that you want for yourself, and not a dress that your friend is wearing. Only then will someday you wear an even better dress and the world will be obsessed with replicating you. He taught me to set a mark for oneself; the kind that reminds us of our worth. And although I call him my brother and disgust him for not speaking much, his actions make him way older and his success makes the silence feel louder. My favorite person is my brother hence; because I have never met another teacher who gave me the lessons that could make a life, rather than build one.

CHAPTER SIXTEEN

WHERE LOVE FINDS YOU WITHOUT WARNING.

The comforting warmth of soft sunshine felt on a chilly winter morning

Where the dense fog swallows the vibrant hues of the day

The essence of forgiveness and the blessing of acceptance

The adamant hope that carries immense faith in a lifeless soul

The sudden dreams that begin to feel real

The kind of sleep that happily invites itself in,this time with no effort

A laughter so loud and pure, it stuns your inner child

A typical kind of assurance that continues to keep you grounded

And a surprising preview which hints at a happy ending

Your own little world and time just slows down it's pace
Devoid of unsolicited judgements and infused with unconditional acknowledgement
Your existence is glorified and you've transformed into someone's reason
Reason that they love to just be, your pain is a punishment to them
Your tears are like needles pricking their skin and causing them to bleed
So you put aside the trauma because the heart wishes for another chance
Call it an experiment you trust, or a result you wait for, but you step in regardless
It feels safer this time, and the scare is only another thrill
If you unnecessarily catch your lips curving outwards as your mind wanders back,
Might just call this a soft brush with love that is true

CHAPTER SEVENTEEN

Sixteen Years of Silence.

Sixteen years is undeniably a very long time to speak of, but regardless I fortunately concluded that I could withstand the most tumultuous times, with a smile that was unbelievable, and a demeanor that was flawless. It was as if I was teaching myself to somehow thrive inside a conflicted and brutally damaged soul, while eventually transforming it into a resistant and indestructible self, which at some point I knew I would refuse to believe in. The irony of it all was the interesting fact that I was capable of stopping the monster without turning myself into one. Although I had fallen victim to hatred and cold-hearted sentences expressing themselves through violent actions, I still take pride in saying that empathy and benevolence yet keep me company. I guess those sixteen years weren't just never-ending months of sorrow and unwanted despair, but a genuinely long enough time to mould me into a tougher self that could stay put through everything, even though slowly withering away.

Sixteen years later, I stumble upon a kind of love that makes me believe in the possibility of permanence, and the achievability of absolute happiness. Sixteen years later I'm told by a stranger that I am worthy of a love that consumes me, and I am capable of being loved generously. Even though the shadows of danger were dancing somewhere in the backdrop of it all, a sliver of hope somehow shown in me, and I held his hand firmly, as if allowing myself to accept the idea that I too was deserving of another chance at living. Walking down the memory lane, I did recall the innumerable days when my hope stemmed up from nothing but lighted candles and habitual prayers, all directed to someone who had never paid me a visit when I looked up to the stars and sobbed silently. Even though I knew none but He had heard me, I had never heard him speak a word that would console me. But exactly sixteen years later I reckon, it was only He who watched it all, and waited for my time to come. Maybe all that emotional outpour was necessary for me to embrace supreme bliss when it came to me.

But then again, my insides were still raw. The wounds are still fresh, and the heart still aces at nights when the stars refuse to show. Every truth somehow hints at a lie, even when there couldn't be the slightest possibility. Every act of acceptance feels like a façade that would soon fade away. Every word of assurance sounds like fabricated half-truths. Even when I know this love is the poetic kind that they write in books, how do I refill the empty void that now screams of insecurities and distrust because of what happened over a period of sixteen long years? Even though I had picked myself up and walked through it all to stand here today, how do I confidently claim that I'm yet again ready to fight a new battle, without knowing what awaits me? Someone told me it takes time to gather yourself. What I fear however is what if it takes me longer than how long the other person is willing to wait for?

I have moved past the falsified version of love that tormented me for sixteen long years, and that I am certain of. But how do I lay faith in the sudden version of unconditional love, knowing all I've ever gotten in return is abandonment? The never-ending fear still holds me back each night, but this time I know I'll conquer it. My only reinforcement is time, and I hope this man offers it to me in abundance, for what I fear the most is to be left stranded with a broken heart, only for not being able to gather myself within the said amount of time. no wonder now I know why the world complains of deadlines!

CHAPTER EIGHTEEN

WHEN LOVE NO LONGER RECOGNIZES ME.

It feels like an enforced solitude, even though I have a hand to hold.

I'm walking along an unmapped route, more like a lost pilgrim in the mountains,

He was just a two-hour flight away from me, yet something stopped me that night.

I felt like a wretched being, as if no ear was eager to listen to what I had to say of life.

I imagined a tomorrow that never came, for life had other things to offer,

And time ran out like pouring sand from between my fingers.

Whenever our eyes met, I found my reflection in him.

But it's now that I fathom, how scarred I have become.

You may call him a lover, but he is a changed man now. As life presented newer challenges, his heart forgot to embrace love; his eyes shined no more, his blood rushed every minute.

They told me I must still stay, for my children want me to.

For the world believes marriages culminate in happiness.

But doesn't that mean the sadness will stay subdued and not leave me forever?

Do I have to hide my unhappiness because the man I loved, doesn't desire me no more?

Do I have to plead for his company; for he feels I'm an invader, a forceful conqueror of his world?

Perhaps the mind will make its way for now, but the soul in me is halfway already.

It will wait for the 'time to sew', until it perishes in hopelessness.

It was two years from now, when my thoughts aligned with his. I was like the light he awaited to see since decades.

Even now I think of our times, hours when he spent looking at me and I said nothing but smiled.

I adore his company I must say, for I'm devoted to his love even today.

Our love feels like the wandering clouds, the freezing cold of December and the lurking flavor of chocolate.

But whenever we are together, something just falls out of place. It's as if he is controlled by the demon, when anger lands on his mind.

We've shifted to mornings when seeing me isn't exciting to him no more, we let go of nights when his last words couldn't make time as he was in the company of 'better' folk.

We ceased from initiating dialogues, for it now looks like a repeating circle.

As I type this in my typewriter, only one thought comes to mind,

Is the longevity of passion just a myth, love a cause of suffering?

I don't know.

Maybe love does endure—but only in memory, not in presence. And maybe that's what hurts the most.

CHAPTER NINETEEN

THE HANDPRINT ON THE WINDOW!

The season of fall whispered a fond adieu as Thanksgiving bid farewell and wintertime knocked on the door. I have seen a thousand seasons come and pass by, as I sat at the corner of my table skimming over "The Snow Child". Back in the days when I was much naïve, I was deluded into believing that Old Man Winter was truly the one who brought in snow and the freezing cold nights. You may say my first love was him, who many now know as Jack Frost. I have always adored the foggy mornings and colder nights; there is something about the shivers that run through the body. Even though my hair has grayed by now, and my fingers tremble as I pick my cup of black coffee, I still envy the silhouetted Christmas tree against the murky, winter sky. At times I'd walk to the other room and listen to "Last Christmas" and "God Rest Ye Merry Gentlemen" on my vinyl record that my beloved Jeremy had gifted me. "Remember Christ our Savior, was born on Christmas Day", was his favorite line. I'm holding on to my glass of cinnamon buttered rum, as I recline in my easy chair. Oh, just so you know, I never cherished alcohol. But alas, my kids impelled me to try. Not to mention, their forever partisan Jeremy, gave in to their cause. Manhattan city turns to a winter wonderland, each time the Christmas bells begin ringing. I'm talking about nearly sixty five years from today, when all four of us roamed the streets of New York, covered from head to toe in coats and boots, but hand in hand. We'd often click photographs, standing in front of the gorgeous Rockfeller Christmas Tree. I could show you the album now, but some pages are blank. I had kept them safe in the bedroom closet but I'd not be able to search it for you, I'm afraid my back hurts. This reminds me of how I used to grow tired and break my back, baking pumpkin pics, cinnamon buns and roasted turkey on every Christmas Eve. They savored my delicacies! I was nonetheless young in those days, but sure they gave me a hard time, until all the chores were over and we huddled in front of the fireplace and shared ghost stories till midnight. Often, the younger one would sing a carol while the elder one mocked him for his voice. Jeremy never rebuked them, he knew it was all for fun. There, that's the fireplace I'm talking of. It's been years now, since I last lit it up. So as I was saying, Jeremy and I would be left there, reminiscing our high school years and the kids would rush out to the front yard and build endless snowmen. I could see them from here, this window. Their happy faces always made me content. By the evening, Manhattan would light up with holiday lights and brim with winter extravaganzas. On some nights, the kids brought in their friends. And we all feasted on pies and cakes. Oh how I adored festivals back in those days, until one fine evening, I could find them no more. They were headed to the Columbus Circle Holiday Market, and I waited for their return. Alas, I never saw them since.

The authorities couldn't find them, and many said they left for the skies. I don't really know the shady truth but I remember I saw a hand impression on the window two days back. I knew it was the younger one's. I know they're playing somewhere nearby and would return to me when its time. The other day, Jeremy had written a letter to me and often sends me more. The only fear I have is if, he still loves me the same for I now wear glasses and my heart feels weak. Nevertheless, I feel him in my memory and that has kept me going since. Oh, there you see! The lights are up, the streets are full. I've always told my kids to celebrate festivals with the family.

Even if I have no one beside me, you must still celebrate with joy. For I believe—they are never too far. Just hidden, like snow before it falls.

WHERE THE SQUIRRELS FOLLOWED-

Unreal as it was, my then overwrought heart was now overwhelmed by a surreal feeling. I was seated in a yogic posture, almost as if imitating the Buddha's quest for nirvana, already conceptualizing the idea of life as nothing but a cycle of our own actions. Though my lids were shut, I could unmistakably gauge the blissful aura of the place I was in. The murmur of a steady flowing stream came from somewhere and the pleasant breeze caused the leaves to flutter at times. Though a sparrow or two chirped once, I knew they were watching me, confused but intent. As I inhaled once again, the air felt divine. I knew the morning air was alluring, but today it felt like the breath of existence.

Within just a year and a half, life took a complete circle from denial to helplessness to numbness. But this morning, a new feeling germinated and I name it, 'the seed of hope'. It all began with an inevitable shutdown of life, when all were forced into the four walls of their homes and the clock ticked by watching the still mountain from outside the bedroom window. The morning sun heralded a new day while the Prussian blue skies summoned lonely nights. Yet a voice inside spoke to me that, 'better days are near'. Three years of campus life in an unexplored city with unfamiliar faces was summarized into a year of online sessions, recordings and exhaustive lectures, until one fine day they announced the final culmination of a chapter. Even then, the face on the other side of the mirror smiled and said, 'This too shall pass'. In the ensuing months, losses happened like changing seasons. Friends turned to unfamiliar faces, lovers let their desire diminish, families wept the untimely end of young and old, experiences became photographs stuck onto scrapbooks, moments unlived were all a blur and days swiftly turned to age-old memories. If anything remained in me, then that was the 'seed of hope'- the subtle ray of optimism that shone bright like the light at the end of a tunnel; the little message hidden inside the half-sunk bottle that read, 'cling on, it's all temporary'.

I inhaled deep. My eyes were still shut but the muscles felt easy and the chest was not tight anymore. I slowly parted my lids and let those eyeballs wander, as I exhaled for the final time. I thought for one last time, "You only fear losing when you're attached to something". No attachments, I repeated to myself.

I didn't have a confidant to make her my human diary, I didn't have a lover who's comforting embrace could soothe my pain, I didn't have a lord who showed me he was there when I mumbled alone to the ceiling, I didn't have a parent who could comprehend my deteriorating mind as months turned to years and I never said a word. But this morning, seed of optimism bore fruition and all the formidable times looked nothing but a short movie, which never really transpired into a reality. I read it correctly, "You are the hope for yourself; you bear the light that must guide you through the kaleidoscope of life. Trust the process of it".

But where did I read it? Was it some ancient novel or an advice an elder had given me? I can feel my fingers shake as I type this; it is me who fathomed it. I got up and placed my feet firmly on the ground, as my toes felt the moist grass underneath. My lips curved into a smile, as I looked up to the sky. It was a shade of bright blue today. I began walking on my way as the little squirrels began to follow.

CHAPTER TWENTY-ONE

THE HALF-SMILE RITUAL.

My morning ritual is usually to wake up and rush to the shower after the regular cup of black tea and think of every plausible or far-fetched circumstance that would in turn wreck havoc in my already shrinking mind, as the cold outpour of water trickles down my face, washing away the free-flowing tears with it. The funniest affair however, that bewilders me almost often, is how a sudden half-smile appears on my lips right after I step out of the bathroom door. It is as if the mind has set it as a custom and the face instantly comprehends the urgency of it. The audience that watches me therefore is easily duped into thinking it's a natural occurrence. Even though I cannot help myself and let out a short laugh, I immediately step back grasping the irony of it. Just like every other morning therefore, I encountered the same episode even today. But surprising as it has been, a sudden stroke of cognition ran over me. And my dear readers consider yourselves fortunate for its early in the day and you already have something to read about! I sometimes wonder if everything that the heart of a writer carries, serves as a feisty content to the reader's curiosity.

Nonetheless, I must continue with my story.

I stepped towards the mirror and looked straight into it. The reflection stared back at me, as if it were a whole another person. I wondered how it had such glimmering, bright eyes that stared at me so intently while my own blinked every nano-second as they struggled to keep still. It was as if a bottle was brimming with water and the liquid would gush out any moment, and yet you try to tighten the cork with might and main, only so not a single drop would spill. Suddenly I could hear footsteps, as if someone was coming to check on me. Not because something could've been unusual, but because a chore needed my notice. I now desperately tried to imitate the reflection, I had to look as fine as it. Suddenly it starts to laugh, more like in a hysterical fashion- as if it was mocking me that my struggle was all in vain.

I sat down on the marbled floor, as I continued to rub those eyes. Horror struck me when they began to swell, what will I answer I wondered. Just then, my cell phone lit up, a friend had written something. "It would've been okay if it was just a phase, but for you it seems like forever", it read. I pondered for a second until I began to comprehend in bits. The reflection was the self that I was yet to become. This existence of today is the consequence of uncertainty and inhibition, a tale of years, a story of a kid.

I shut my eyes and plug in the earphones. Didn't they say music was an escape? In an instant, I traveled to a world that was yet all fiction. Perhaps fiction was now my only tranquilizer until reality brought me the comfort that I'm yet in a search for.

And as the music swelled, I let myself drift away—into the fiction where my heart found a moment's peace.

CHAPTER TWENTY-TWO

2555 DAYS TO REUNION.

Disguised as an idiosyncratic private eye in that shiny black overcoat and a fedora hat, As if I had just come out of a James Bond movie and now geared up for late night shenanigans, Breathing in the icy winds as the blizzards gained pace, The slushy, deserted streets of Manhattan city saw none but me.

My buckle heavy Gothic boots amplified the sound of the otherwise steady footsteps, Tonight I was off to meet a long lost friend, nearly a round of 2555 days until our fortunes lit up our lives.

Connery might mistake me as his lookalike for I must camouflage myself from the formidable curse of the rabble, who despised desire for an exiled lover.

Exactly 2555 days from tonight, we had set out on divergent paths, only to reunite on the day we find the purpose.

Tonight is the day when I shall introduce myself as a tycoon, and she an acclaimed songbird. I could now see a young maiden walk towards me, biting her pale white lips as she always would.

Dressed in shimmery blue, as her neat curls fluttered in the gusts of wind, Oh she looked nothing but my Elsa and this time I couldn't "let it go".

As she stepped closer holding my hand with hers, my half frozen body suddenly came back to life, Just like a prolonged dry spell in the Sahara quenches its yearlong thirst once the skies begin to pour.

Or like a lost child in a busy fair who finally gets to see his mother, She was the warmth I awaited since all these years and tonight it seemed nothing but serene.

As my lips touched hers, a fire lit up within, as if the heart was dead until now, thriving and alive. As the blizzard turned to sleet, we stood there still.

We could be buried in the snow only to reincarnate as Kristof and Elsa, only to unbind our kingdom of love from the grip of timeless winter.

This time I wouldn't keep undercover neither would she be trapped faraway else, We shall endure the stumbling blocks until time summons us to the churchyard.

Tonight, beneath the endless winter sky, we rewrite our fate- no longer shadows, but the architects of our own forever.

CHAPTER TWENTY-THREE

THE POET'S REALISM.

Tonight my pages seem devoid of worthy phrases, the ink in my pen refuses to spill out.

I wonder if my mind has given up on artistry, until I realize it's the bitter taste of realism I must embrace.

Poets often imagine utopian scenery, existing in extremes of either love or hate,

But this night I failed to envision one, for I knew now that the world couldn't be perfect.

I had stumbled upon persons of different hues; some lived to laugh while others envied the end.

But little did I learn, every affinity had a lesson to teach.

Some became my confidants; I named some others as soul mates.

Some fell in love with me, while others feared my vulnerability.

They all stayed until a time had come, when reality revealed in phases.

Some let go of their customary wisdom, while some turned unfamiliar to me.

Each had a reason to speak of, but I knew I was a loner now.

The one lesson I wrote down, was to never again let an alien know me,

For I could never tell, when a friend turns to foe,

And so tonight I'm at a loss of phrases, words or any poetry,

For I cannot elucidate upon unreal love, imperishable friendships and shatterproof hearts,

I cannot recite a malicious poem, which paints a perfect abode of man.

Though I still hold on to my pen, I know not a word is left to be told.

Tonight, the pen rests — not from lack of will, but from the weight of truths that silence even the fiercest muse.

CHAPTER TWENTY-FOUR

BETWEEN TIME AND TIDE.

Unshackled in a flash and pushed aside, I fell to my knees as the clock struck twelve,
An unfinished tale of 518 days, this half broken, time worn castle subsumed my tears and unheard screams.
I looked out the casement window that eyed the waters; the tranquil night had summoned me,
I held on to my pale blue sundress as I hurried towards the abandoned tower,
The glimmering moonlight guided my way as the crystal blue ocean watched me arrive.
I sat down feeling the cold desert underneath my bruised feet, the serene waves crashing against the shore,
As my eyes met each other, I was overcome by a flurry of unlived moments.
An afternoon spent in a tree house or a soiree in a deserted machan,
A casual walk by the blue green waters underneath the moon or a lonely night in a stranded island,
A two-wheeler ride along winding hilly roads in sunless mornings and blurred landscapes,

Make love amidst the deepest woods whilst the mighty wolves howl at a distance,
Pitch tents in some remote valley or just sit by the fire and jam to blues in a fine December,
Sit beside a deserted lake and watch the pebbles scare the birds away,
Hour-long drives to vintage lands and lip-syncing Don Williams,
Or perhaps wear a flower crown and go missing in Bordeaux,
I open my eyes to feel the same breeze, the ocean listening to my reverie.
I leaned back and watched the sky, the stars shining just the same,
The only change was in the contrasting time,
One that set me free and the other that bound me to confinement.
I left behind a life that I could pen down in the testaments,
for amusement was new to me, until time confined me.

CHAPTER TWENTY-FIVE

WHAT IF I MEET YOU AGAIN?

Come the month of blossom and the caress of the wind reminds me of your touch,

I've lived a thousand seasons alone but fancied welcoming the daffodils with you.

My feathered friends have been sharing the language of love, they lend me a hint but I assure it's tough.

The sky seems sanguine, glistening in crimson

I succumb to its memory, for I haven't watched them ever alone.

The waters resembled a crystal; I could mistake it for a mirror.

I walked past it all with an iffy heart, what if once again it stumbled upon you?

CHAPTER TWENTY-SIX

A LONER'S SOLACE.

Overcast morns and befuddled minds,

Fathomless woods enshrouded in the overlaying mist.

Numb feet impassive to the moist turf,

The distant cheep of the winter finch.

An unhurried walk in the absence of warmth,

Occasional puffs of air as the lips slightly part,

Colorless hours awaiting the sunrise,

I see a lost maiden amidst the swarm of souls, she smiles

A word or two, her voice timorous

She resembled a façade of comfort, the reality was in disguise

That heart sparkled, underneath the graying clouds

It seemed that wind suited her, if not the mortals.
    Was this a loner's solace I wondered.

If yes, how eccentric yet special it was!

CHAPTER TWENTY-SEVEN

DROWN ME IN THE BLUES.

Sing to me your dulcet lullaby, let that euphonious strain set my afflicted soul to peace,

For tonight I decide to drown myself amidst the intimidating surge of the blues,

At a time when the sun resolves to die and the moonlight takes its first breath.

This enervated heart of mine is too frail to resist the tides of gloom,

It has now chosen the omnipotent silence as its eternal resting home.

Tonight, I surrender—to the hush, the blues, and the lullaby that never ends.

CHAPTER TWENTY-EIGHT

SOMEWHERE BETWEEN MARCH AND OCTOBER.

The date etched in my memory is the 15th of March, 2020—though it was past midnight, so technically, the 16th.

Even though slightly ambivalent, I fully loathed this hour and felt overwhelmed by a fresh sweep of rancor, thinking it was all predestined and perhaps was nothing but a consequence of my own deeds, probably I was too happy to discern the outcomes that might follow. There it was, clear and all in place, he was leaving the next morning. It was the born day of one of my most intimate pals the next day and it was seldom that I wasn't exuberant enough for the same. This time, it seemed absolute grey to me, I was dispirited and lamenting whatever was just playing out in front of me.

He kept assuring me, 'Just fifteen days, darling. I'll be back before you miss me.' But how do I explain to you—the reader—the storm that brewed inside me?

Well, I feel I owe my readers an explanation at this stage so they know the root to my musings and contemplation. The title I owned was something most of you might connect with. Its termed "over thinking" that literally translates into over-scrutinizing events or happenings. I excelled in this regard and hence, it is needless to say that I could foresee the ensuing future crystal clear (even though my over-analyzing mind could not succeed in predicting the petrifying repercussions of a miniscule virus!). I kept on trying to convince him that things weren't supposedly staged to happen the way he had scripted them to. Nevertheless, I was time and again overlooked and after a point I started sketching myself this falsified version of romance in which things gradually decided to look hearty and just.

I shall not misinform my readers by suggesting that our bond was supposedly dull and grey, it wasn't. There were innumerable instances if I am to narrate, when he's stirred me a wholesome delicacy or probably surprised me with not-so-extravagant gifts (May I call it a reason big enough that made my heart skip its beat whenever he picked up the word "distance" from his love imbued glossary? Or was I just too half hearted to usher it in, knowing I would be incapable of cultivating it?). Well, I shall now furnish my tale in a more precise form.

The backdrop is reminiscent of the most abysmal times that set the stage for the novel virus to take birth. Needless to say, all workplaces came to a halt and hence we were left with no other possibility but to set for home. He was the first one to stand firm on such a settlement and was to leave for the mountains in the morning of 16th March. It's of that day that I choose to narrate. I must clarify herein that it isn't a remembrance of heartbreak or a grief laden plot of love, rather it's a hint toward the ambiguity of life and the sudden alterations of living that can forever haunt you for laying faith in the repeated phrase of taking your existence "for granted".

I remember being overburdened with sleep when one of my eyes merely struggled to open. (We had promised each other to not succumb to demanding exhaustion and instead live through the entire night, talking and listening to melodies that celebrated romance). The song that night could give you chills if you were to dance in tandem with its soothing rhythm beside the beach with your lover's hand in yours. I shall read out the name to my readers as well so they don't deprive themselves of this blissful chance to render such a heartfelt music to their ears: Wherever you go by Mark Knophler.

I cannot recall how and when my eyes just decided to meet and sleep slowly creped in (no wonder I still regret the uninvited and unwanted bane). People in love would connect when I say there's a completely different satiation when you are in an aura of godly affection and soft music assures you of eternity and you just thank your guardian angel in a silent sense and do nothing but smile at how merciful the almighty has been to you. I was a victim of undivided love and hence perhaps, I couldn't help but fall prey to the beauty of it all.

It was a 6 AM flight to Assam and I don't question your ability in knowing that early morning flights need you to curse your precious sleep and rush to the airport at an hour when the world is perhaps seeing their first dream!

As I struggled to make sense of what was actually going on around me, with the blurred vision due to my sleepy eyes, I felt him come close to me and plant a soft kiss on my forehead "My cab is waiting honey, I'll call you soon".
I was about to sit up straight, my head bursting in pain and my eyes yet to clearly make sense of the small room that just had a dim light on, when he caressed my face and whispered "Sleep, I'll call you".

Writing all this, I have no understanding or knowledge if I'm even slightly successful in making my readers realize how ugly that morning looked to me and why. Perhaps all I can do is paint a tranquil imagery in front of your eyes, where you picture two souls immersed in the drug of love, thankful to their ancestors for the present they behold and the bliss that translates into utter adoration for each other's existence. And then in a twinkle of an eye, you realize it slipping away from your frame of utopian living and all that's left to sense or see is obscurity.

I pushed myself up and embraced him in whatever strength I had. If only I held the boon to keep him this close to me for every two minutes of separation he'd ask for. I don't remember next.

I finally woke up when the sun shone bright and the empty room reminded me of the loneliness I was to adopt and this time, it wasn't any usual alarm but his phone call that said "I reached, hope you're fine".

We've been together in this city for over a year now and

I just couldn't come to terms with the realization that we are miles apart from each other, hoping to meet sometime soon. (I was seldom allowed to venture out with friends back home and hence somewhere I knew, this meet would take time).

He said it would be fifteen days and now I'm here,, writing this brief story of a time when my life was probably a little more merciful and bestowed on me the biggest blessings I could ever ask for, and when I glance at my phone for a second, probably because some notification popped up, I realize it's the 2nd of October, 2020. "Six months already?" I let out an uncomfortable smile.

"2021 would definitely see us together" a faint ray of hope reassured my thoughts that were once again crystal clear that "it is here to stay". Lord, forgive my preoccupied mind!

CHAPTER TWENTY-NINE

A Journey Through Pain, Realization, and Hope.

Prologue: The Silent Summit

Gazing at the eternal mountaintop- so eerily reminiscent of the Sierra in America- I settled my skeptical mind. Winter had already taken its seat, and the somber essence of a sunless morning seemed to weaken me. They say my words can weave endless tales, but today, I am at a sheer loss. A loss of words. A loss of breath. A loss of self.

What I share now is not just a story- it's a lived experience. One laced with grief, regret, and a bitter taste of reality. A story I hope will show that permanency is an illusion and contentment, scarred.

The First Trigger: A Pain Revisited

I had to visit Kolkata about a month ago for an urgent matter. My mother was hesitant about taking me, but some situations simply demand companionship. After reaching,

I experienced an alarming chest pain. A pain I had known since childhood- one that had always been dismissed as mere gastritis.

But this time, it was different. I couldn't breathe. My mother panicked. We were alone in a city that didn't know us. Due to COVID protocols, no doctor agreed to see me immediately. The pain lingered for two days until we finally got an appointment and I was prescribed an ultrasound.

Diagnosis and Disillusionment

The ultrasound results left me numb. I was diagnosed with multiple calculi in the gall bladder- acute cholelithiasis. There was no space left in the organ. I tried to seek reassurance from my friend- a childhood confidante and a biology student.

"They'll give you medicines. Just don't stress."

I trusted her. But when the doctor finally explained the gravity of the situation, my world paused. Surgery was immediate. Delays could cause the bladder to burst. But we weren't in Kolkata long enough. So, we returned to Assam, hoping to act swiftly.

Reality Check: The Illusion of Youth

Coming home felt like a return to safety. But not for long. Tests began. New revelations surfaced—a fatty liver, elevated enzymes, and more complications. I didn't drink, didn't smoke, didn't live irresponsibly. Yet here I was.

This irony stung: I was young, seemingly vibrant on the outside, but my internal world was crumbling. My heart ached not just physically- but emotionally. I had begun mourning parts of myself I hadn't even lived fully yet.

The Diwali Breakdown: A Night of Lights and Darkness

Diwali arrived. Our home was glowing with fairy lights, but my soul was too broken to celebrate. I clutched my chest as pain returned with ruthless force. I vomited water, peed blood, and nothing stayed inside me. Medications failed. I begged for death. The surgeon called me into emergency.

I somehow walked into the ER- without a wheelchair- and collapsed on the bed. Painkillers flooded my veins. My mother's teary eyes silently prayed. Slowly, I calmed. I was discharged- but the war was far from over.

The Final Blow: COVID

Just a day before my surgery, the unimaginable happened.

"You're COVID positive," they said.

I couldn't believe it. Neither could my family. The surgery was postponed. I was isolated, my pain left untreated, my faith shaken. And then, three days later, my mother tested positive too.

Even nightmares hadn't painted this version of my life.

Solitude and Self-Realization

In this silence, with no music to soothe me and no strength to speak, I realized how deeply I was aching. Not just in my body, but in my mind. A thousand thoughts rang in my head. Was it the virus that worsened everything? Did I bring this misfortune home?

But I've stopped trying to find blame.

Instead, I write. I pen this all down not to gain sympathy, but to make sense of it all. To remind myself- and perhaps you- that this year hasn't just been a curse. It has also been a blessing in disguise.

Closing Reflections: The Meaning of Life

Life isn't in the grand things. It isn't just in walks along empty streets with music or treks to mountain heavens. It's not in accolades, love stories, or success.

Life is in the reflection you smile at in the mirror, and the struggle to protect that smile. That's where life truly resides.

2020 broke me, taught me, and molded me. It showed me the fragility of existence and the strength of the human spirit. And above all, it revealed this truth: even pain can birth a kind of peace.

CHAPTER THIRTY

THE SILENT SEED: A FATHER'S LOVE IN SHADOWS.

The Dawning of an Infant

The dawning of an infant is like the blossoming of a seed. It's an unknown sphere, marked by the curiosities of existence and peculiar customs. As the newborn opens his eyes to see the subtleties of his surroundings, he finds himself extremely vulnerable to every detail of the human world.

He is deeply cared for, and his family is immensely passionate about his every minute detail—from the delightful and endearing smile that his soft lips make, to his habitual babbling. The day he finally spells out the monosyllable "mom," it's the most treasured moment for the mother. The father smiles from the side, so pleased with his life and this precious gift he's been bestowed with.

He is aware that he is not introduced as an affectionate and subtle-natured being in the titles. However, he is more than content to work hard and furnish his child with the finest life.

Have You Seen the Seed Grow?

Daily care—light, water, nutrients. A beautiful flower germinates. Correspondingly, the child grows into an adult. He begins to perceive the world around him and starts to mold the possibilities to suit his determination and impetus.

In this entire journey, he comes across unexpected ordeals: guilt, heartbreaks, confusion, instability, and regret. Yet, he continues to sail through.

Remember the seed? Dust and heavy storms ordained the plant to bow down. Yet, it stood firmly and looked ever natural. Beautiful.

A Silent Pillar of Love

Amidst all the hustle, there's one pillar that stands strong. The world reveres it as motherly love. But did they ever teach us about the paternal warmth? What it feels like to acknowledge a father's selfless efforts?

No.

Hard times came and went. He found himself a lover for an eternity and was blessed with an offspring. Take a pause here—the roles have changed. He's a father himself now.

All his life, the man who was just a means to expropriate financial benefits from has begun to acquire the status of a respectable being. The reason? He has come to be susceptible to that similar stress of running an entire family, making sure his loved ones have everything they cherish, and shedding his blood and tears just to see a smile on their faces.

No. He isn't supposed to get appreciated for making this tremendous benefaction.

Decline

In his declining years, the father was overwhelmed by a chronic disease. The medical practitioners gave up on hope, and the staunch, enigmatic man was reduced to nothing but a replica of a skeleton.

His body shrunk each day. His hair fell off. His hands were shaky. His legs trembled. He fumbled upon words and could not recall a person.

They went to see him. He was shaken by the horrifying visual. Never could he imagine in his entirety that someday, he would see his father look at him as an alienic being—and just sit and stare. Not talk.

He did give money for his recovery. But what about the guilt that he was overridden with?

The Call

One morning, when he woke up to reach for his coffee, his cell popped up a missed call.

The doctors called to say his father was no more.

Silence.

Four Years Later

It has been four years since his father's demise.

He looks at his picture and speaks indistinctly to himself:

"How do I make up for the times we did not sit together to share a cup of coffee and talk about world affairs?

How do I tell people that I'm left with no memories of you because all that mattered was my business and not asking you how you were?

How do I do away with the guilt of never recognizing your existence and valuing your sweat for my elitist future?

You left me with no answers, Pa."

Sigh.

CHAPTER THIRTY-ONE

WHEN I FOUND MYSELF.

The unending battle of a million differences seemed an idiosyncratic trait of mine, until the story of 21 long years finally culminated into a neat epilogue.

The blazing sun had bid me farewell and the setting dusk took over.

I picked up my stylograph dipped in the bottle of ink but did not let it feel the coarse paper.

If I were an artist, I would have painted you in a mosaic of shades, both bright and somber.

The hour of shadows was nothing but gloomy until you taught me to chase them.

Sunsets invited a colorless sky until you showed me the shades of lilac and crimson.

I did not see a lover in you nor did I ever spill my truths out to you.

Perhaps, thy Lord had sensed it years ago that my search was meant for something else.

As I lean back on the chair and the welcoming breeze brushes through my face, I close my eyes gently.

They were feeling heavy until now. I watch myself travel through time, transcending the boundaries of despair and a broken heart.

Idyllic as you may call it, I was now in a world of smiles.

You stood at a distance and waved at me. That smile seemed holy and I stepped back a little, perfection was only a realization as I recalled.

Just then, in a blink of an eye, you came closer and whispered a holy spell- "life is too beutiful to be wasted fighting every battle".

I turned to see but you were long gone. All that remained was a note on the ground.

Was it some mystery I was asked to fathom or was it me untangling my chaos?

I'm opening my eyes for now I know my fountain pen has pages to fill.

I know the process is slow but I had the shield in me.

Maybe happiness is this- when I found myself!

In Praise Of A Dying Habit A Writer's Reflection.

During my years as a school-going kid, we were assigned 'summer-reading projects', in which we had to create detailed reports on a book that we were asked to read. Often times, our teachers would give out a printed sheet, which had the list of books mentioned, and the bookstores from where we could get them. Needless to say, these books were generally short stories, but most often, they were also well-known novels, like those of 'Oliver Twist', and 'David Copperfield', or even Mark Twain's classics. Even though there was a group of students who disgusted these projects, nevertheless a majority of them turned out with highly creative reports, decorated with all kinds of fancy materials, and stylized fonts. Often times, it was hard to discern if it was solely a child's effort, or if a parent had offered a helping hand. Nevertheless, such projects were extremely exciting. We eventually started to maintain our own collections, and would often boast of the new fiction that our parents got us from the yearly book fairs in town. Back in those days, students like us visited the book fairs out of natural curiosity. They wanted to get hold of the latest fiction, the funniest comics, sketchbooks, non-fiction, biographies, and even cook-books. Fast forward to a few years, it pains my heart as I see the tradition fading away. To speak of myself, even though I claim to be a passionate story-teller, it wasn't before the virus locked me in, that I decided to actually put my thoughts on paper. Back in my school years, we had a specific period in the time table, marked out for the library. Although half of the students considered it a 'free class'', there were some book geeks who waited eagerly for the class to begin. They would enter the library, and head straight to the shelves to borrow the stories that would keep them through the weekends. Yet some others crouched up in front of their school bags placed on the desk, and read novels like they'd devour a new delicacy. In those times, such students were admonished for reading novels during class. I used to have a friend who was addicted to English classics. This meant that there were strict rules regarding turning pages, bending the books, using a book mark, and keeping it safe in the study, until the day you decide to return it, out of annoyance! These books were like the medicines that came with caution – 'keep away from the reach of children, and store in a cool, dark place'.

As I write about those golden times, I realize how the 'reading culture' has gradually died out. I wish to talk about two very important things here. Firstly, people in the contemporary world barely have time to go through a newspaper or an autobiography of a renowned personality. Until and unless it is a magazine with a visual appeal, or bearing some scandal or buzz about a fashion celebrity, people seldom bother to flip through the pages. What amazes me is the fact that, I am not talking of a massive generation gap here. Even then, it seems like the 'reading generation' is fading out. The content that is today spanning the reading market, barely has any space left for mythology, science fiction, visionary and philosophical titles, mystery, thrillers, and even poetry. I am not generalizing this condition in any way, but on the flipside, this is gradually becoming a reality. Even though there is a particular section of common folk who relate to verses, epigrams, or lyrics of a song, one would seldom find houses which have bookshelves stacked with novels, or even comics for that matter. A few scrolls through social media applications satiate their urge to sync their thoughts with relatable words, and that compensates for poetry books or even anthologies. Gone are the days when magic and JK Rowling gripped minds in an instant, the simplistic details of nature by Ruskin Bond enticed readers in a second, and the edgy thrillers of Satyajit Ray hooked you to your seats. In this age of transition, writers are made to write for the market, and not for their creative inclinations. Writing has become more of a 'relatable' tale, than that of a creative avenue. People do visit book fairs even today, but the reason hasn't remained the same anymore. From a place to find and discover newer stories, it has now turned to a place meant for an informal social gathering, and a fun evening coupled with food and whispers. The habit of reading is gradually waning out. As a writer myself, it pains me to see that even publishers are selective of only those pieces which they think have a space in the 'modern market'. In such a 'competitive space' where writers are not inventing stories but competing for a niche, we are losing quality content. The trend has therefore shifted to non-fiction. Even though, the idea of self-publishing has opened up newer avenues for debut authors who are coming up with creative stories, the final support rests with the readers. There still exists a significant section of people, who find it hard to believe that some books can be worth their time.

After reading several biographies of successful authors, it is now that I reckon why they shifted to writing as a hobby. None of them took writing as a full-fledged career option, and the real reason remains the fluctuations in the reading audience and their choice of content. There stands no surety that a book is going to top the lists until and unless it meets the tastes of the reader. But then again, if photography, art, dance, and music can pay well, why can't writing do the same? Perhaps because the general perception has increasingly aligned writing with academics, and the subjectivity of creativity has essentially become its deterrent. However I shall clearly state at the same time, that this isn't a global phenomenon, as book clubs still function outside my country, in full swing. Reading sessions and poetry recitations are still a thing in some places. The difference lies in their magnitude and span.

Nevertheless, I am still hopeful of a time when people would prefer the fresh smell of a new book, to that of an electronic document file of a story. I am still hopeful that, people will someday acknowledge the essence of creativity, and not limit it to cliché categories. However along with this realization, there also has to emerge a new group of creators, story-tellers, and writers, who would invent and explore, rather than imitate and continue. Literature is a rich repository of creativity, and we must not let it go waste.